Real Spirit

Fun ideas for refreshing, relaxing, and staying strong

By Elizabeth Chobanian
Illustrated by Carol Yoshizumi

Published by Pleasant Company Publications

Questions or comments? Call 1-800-845-0005,
visit our Web site at **americangirl.com,**
or write American Girl, P.O. Box 620497, Middleton, WI 53562-0497.

Printed in China.
05 06 07 08 09 10 C&C 10 9 8 7 6 5 4 3 2 1

American Girl® is a registered trademark of American Girl, LLC.

Editorial Development: Elizabeth Chobanian, Michelle Watkins,
Therese Maring, Patti Kelley Criswell

Art Direction and Design: Chris Lorette David

Production: Kendra Schluter, Mindy Rappe, Jeannette Bailey, Judith Lary

Illustrations: Carol Yoshizumi

Photography: cover, pp. 43–61—Christopher Zweifel at Quad Photo; p. 8, 31, 33, 40—Fotosearch;
p. 7, 13, 16, 29, 30, 32, 35, 37, 41—Corbis; p. 1—Creatas

This book is not intended to replace the advice of or treatment by physicians, psychologists, or other experts.
It should be considered an additional resource only. Questions and concerns about mental or physical health should
always be discussed with a doctor or other health-care provider.

Cataloging-in-Publication Data available from Library of Congress.

Dear Reader,

You've heard people use the word *spirit* in all kinds of ways. Cheerleaders have team spirit (yes, they do!), people can have holiday spirit, or you may tell someone "That's the spirit!" when they cheerfully take on an extra-hard task.

At American Girl, we think your *real spirit* is the part of yourself, deep inside, that gives you strength and keeps you balanced when life feels overwhelming. Real spirit is what you need to get through the really tough times.

This book gives you fun ways to relax and re-energize. But yoga poses and bubble baths can't do all the work. You have to pay attention to your body's stress signals, think through problems, and come up with a plan for dealing with them.

So take time to read these ideas and think up some of your own. That's a great first step. Tend to your own real spirit, and you'll be ready to take on challenges that come your way.

Your friends at American Girl

contents

finding balance . . . 6

Your feelings

Dark cloud or silver lining?

Tune in

You have power

starting fresh . . . 12

Get your sleep

Eat right

Quiz: Wise about exercise?

Let it out

STOP!

How do you cope?

Make a plan

boosting your spirit . . . 28

Fun ways to feel better fast!

soothing and strengthening . . . 42

Mmm . . . massage

Mmmore massage

Imagine

Yoga for you

Big truth

finding balance

Listen to your body's signals and stay steady.

Your feelings

In your life, there will be times—both good and bad—when you may feel anxious. Planning a party can be just as stressful as a pop quiz. When the pressure's on, you react physically and emotionally. Your feelings send a warning to your brain and body: "Get ready!" It puts you on alert so that you're ready to take on the challenge.

Dark cloud or silver lining?

Sometimes you may do very well under pressure. Other times you may feel as though you're about to explode. Your response depends on how you feel.

If you're excited about a challenge, such as getting the lead in the school play, you may look at all your responsibilities and feel energized and inspired. But if you're trying to learn your lines when you just had a fight with a friend, your life may feel overwhelming, maybe even out of control. That's when stress becomes harmful.

Tune in

How do you know when you're overwhelmed?
You might notice some of these symptoms:

Body—you're

tired all the time.

having trouble breathing.

getting tense muscles and sweaty hands.

trembling.

breaking out in a rash.

having trouble sleeping.

hungry all the time.

not hungry at all.

Emotions—you feel

irritable.

angry.

frustrated.

worried.

sad.

unable to laugh.

Mind—you have

difficulty concentrating.

trouble remembering.

racing thoughts.

a hard time making decisions.

You have power

You have what it takes to make it through all kinds of difficult times. In the chapters ahead, we'll tell you about the tools you need to keep your spirit strong. Remember, **even if you can't control the things around you, you can control your reaction to them.**

When I start to feel stressed, I try to stop the feelings. I sit down, get a drink, and tell myself, "I can do it. I can get through this." It works!

Karylle, age 11

starting fresh

Feeling good starts with taking care of your body and talking about what's on your mind.

Get your sleep

Sleep helps your body recover from one day and gear up for the next. Most girls need at least nine to ten hours of sleep each night. Try this: On the weekend, count how many hours you sleep before you naturally wake up without an alarm. Try to get this same amount of sleep each night.

If worries are keeping you awake, put them on paper and stop them from racing around in your head. Make a "To Do" list or write in your journal before turning out the light.

Caffeine is a chemical that affects your body the same way that stress does. So if your goal is relaxation, steer clear of caffeine. It's found in coffee, teas, sodas, chocolate, and even in some bottled waters.

Create a bedtime routine. Your body will recognize the routine as a signal that it's time to wind down. Try to keep to the same bedtime every night. Before you settle in, do a number of things in the same order, such as brushing your teeth, setting out your clothes for the next day, and snuggling in bed with a book.

Eat right

Cooking, baking, and sharing meals with friends and family can be great ways to unwind. Here are some tips for keeping your food habits healthy:

1

Eat breakfast. Refuel when you wake up. Eating breakfast will keep you alert throughout the morning.

2

Eat **well-balanced meals** that include fruits, veggies, whole grains, legumes (beans) and proteins, and low-fat dairy products. To grow up healthy, you need all of these.

3 Drink up! Your body needs plenty of water each day. Carry a water bottle with you and fill it up throughout the day.

4 Try not to overdo sugar. The effects of sweet treats on your body are similar to the effects of stress. A "sugar high" is hard on your body and will leave you feeling tired.

5 Grab healthy snacks. Fill a bowl with fruit and cut-up veggies. Then, when you get the munchies, a healthy choice will be right at your fingertips.

6 Slow down! Don't shovel your food; savor it. Pay attention to the taste and texture of each bite. Try not to do other things while you eat—like watching TV or using the computer. Instead, focus on enjoying your meal.

Wise about exercise?

Answer these quiz questions and find out.

1 Taking your dog for a run around the block will make Rover happy. Even after a bad day at school, it'll probably put you in a better mood, too.

True or False?

2 Brisk exercising right before bedtime will make you tired, and you'll fall asleep better.

True or False?

3 You must exercise continuously for at least 30 minutes for it to have any good effect.

True or False?

4 Exercise can release built-up stress in your body.

True or False?

1. True. Get active, and you'll probably notice that you end your workouts in a good mood. That's because exercise causes your body to produce endorphins, chemicals that naturally relax you and lift your spirits.

2. False. Exercise can actually energize you, making it harder to fall asleep. So avoid working out within three hours before bedtime.

3. False. A short walk can go a long way toward keeping you fit. Split a 30-minute routine into three 10-minute mini workouts, and you'll get almost the same benefits. So take the stairs, shoot some hoops— the important thing is to stay active.

4. True. When you're under stress, your body releases hormones that help get you ready to deal with a crisis. If the stress doesn't stop, these hormones continue to circulate in your body, making you tired and lowering your defenses against illness. Exercise helps your body remove these extra hormones.

Let it out

Talk it out.

A heart-to-heart talk with somebody you trust can help pinpoint what's bothering you. So open up to your mom or dad, sister or friend, and share everything that's on your mind.

Write it out.

A journal is a great place to explore your feelings. Sometimes it's hard to make sense of what you're feeling until you write your thoughts down on paper.

Cry it out.

It's absolutely O.K. to cry, since that's your body's way of releasing stress and tension. If you need a shoulder to cry on, ask for one. Just remember, tears alone don't let people know what's bothering you— and how they can help. You need to tell them.

Reach out.

Stress can seriously affect your health. You may not be able to sleep or eat. Your heart may beat fast, or it may be hard to catch your breath. You may have feelings of deep sadness, fear, frustration, or anger. Tell yourself that you're going to be O.K.—but don't stop there. Talk to a parent or teacher about your feelings. Have an adult help you decide if you should see a doctor.

Ask for help.

Stress is sneaky. Sometimes it may seem as if there's no reason at all for your stressful feelings. That doesn't matter. Asking for help when you need it is what strong, smart people do.

Sometimes you just have to . . .

Are you too busy? Do weekends feel just as hectic as weekdays? Are you not really having much fun?

You may be doing too much and not giving your body and mind time to re-energize. If you are consistently tired and stressed out, your schedule may need an overhaul. You might need to quit some activities. But honestly, that isn't the end of the world.

If I'm busy for a few weeks,
I tell myself "I got myself into this," take a deep
breath, and keep my eyes on my goal.
But if it has been going on for months,
I ask "Am I enjoying myself?"
If you're not enjoying things, you should stand up
for yourself and change what you're doing!
Sam, age 14

It's important to keep the commitments you make—if you joined the team, try to finish the season. Then focus on doing a few things well and having time to relax.

You have your whole life to try new things—pace yourself!

How do you cope?

Girls share their own techniques for beating stress.

I try to stop the stress by telling my mom I can only do one thing at a time. She slows down, and then I can, too.

Natalie, age 9

I visualize myself getting my work done successfully. I use this with schoolwork and horse shows.

Emma, age 11

When I'm stressed, I think about all the good things happening this week.

Erin, age 12

Sometimes I draw what I am thinking,
and I think about things
while I am doing it.
Morgan, age 11

I sit on my swing and listen
to music with headphones
and sing along.
It always helps!
Lisa, age 13

I read a book—something that
will make me forget everything
except the story.
Sereena, age 10

When I am stressed and
no one is around to hang out
with, I write in my journal. It's just
like talking to a friend.
Bailey, age 13

Make a plan

Are you worrying too much? Do you need to get some exercise or more sleep? Use this space to write out your plan for feeling better.

boosting your spirit

Fun ways to feel better fast!

1 Get quiet.

Inside, look for a peaceful place in the house with no distractions and not much noise—just a cozy space for you, a soft blanket, and your thoughts. Outside, take a back-to-nature approach by cloud-gazing in the backyard or walking in the park.

2 Nature sounds.

The *whoosh* of ocean waves or the soft sound of falling rain can melt away stress. Throw open a window, close your eyes, and listen to the outdoors. If all you hear is traffic, take a trip to the library. Ask for recordings of environmental sounds. The music of nature—whether it's a babbling brook or rain-forest birds—might relax you right to sleep.

31

3 Clean up.

It's hard to clear your mind—or feel in control—when you're surrounded by junk. Get organized! Put your stuff away. Get rid of things you no longer need. If your space is organized, you'll feel more relaxed.

4 **Make your space meaningful.** Fill your room with pictures, quotes, posters, and cutouts from magazines showing people, places, and things that inspire you. Display pictures of your friends and family. Even when you want to be by yourself, seeing their faces will be a feel-good reminder of their love.

5 Escape from media madness.

From scary movies to depressing news, TV is filled with images that are anything but relaxing. And some computer chat can be downright toxic. Avoid what's negative on TV and the Internet, or just turn them off altogether. See if you notice a difference in how you feel.

6 Music is a great way to relax. **Some kinds of music, such as classical, have been shown to reduce stress levels. Whatever your taste, play what you like. If a song comes on the radio that upsets you, change the station. Play music that soothes you and makes you happy.**

7 Spray a piece of paper or a handkerchief with your favorite scent. Tuck it into your backpack so that you can reach for quick comfort throughout the day.

8 Reset your clock radio alarm so that you wake to music instead of beeping.

9 Take a bath or shower to soothe away the day's worries. Use a lavender-scented body wash for an extra-calming effect.

10

Cuddle up with a pet. Pets give warmth and comfort, and, best of all, they love you no matter what!

11

Start a craft project. Whether you make a friendship bracelet or a handmade card, don't judge yourself. Just put your heart into it!

12 **Dance. Put on your favorite music and get moving!**

13 **If the state of the world is stressing you out, do something about it!** Write a letter to your principal, your mayor, or even the president. Volunteer your time to a good cause. Helping others will help you feel better, too.

14 **Make music.** Sing, play your violin, or grab your little brother and play karaoke.

15

Share some talent. Show your sister how to kick a soccer ball or help a friend with her homework.

16 The power of touch can make your day! So the next time you're stressed, **ask someone you love for a hug.**

soothing and strengthening

Discover how to refresh and energize using techniques from massage to yoga.

Mmm . . . massage

Muscles tighten when you're stressed. Try these self-massage techniques to loosen up and let go of tension.

Head and Neck

1 Rest your elbows on a flat surface.

2 Place your head in your hands, letting the weight of your head be supported by your fingers.

3 Starting at your hairline, move your fingertips in small circles, working your hands toward the back of your head.

4 When you reach your neck, use two or three fingers on each hand to massage muscles.

Hint: The scent of lavender is said to be stress-busting, so use a lavender-scented lotion or massage oil on your hands when massaging sore muscles.

Mmmore massage

Shoulders

1 Place your right hand on your left shoulder.

2 Using your fingertips, apply pressure in small circles.

3 Then, grasp your shoulder in your hand and knead muscles.

4 Do the same with your left hand on your right shoulder.

Imagine

Relax by using your imagination. Just close your eyes and visualize!

1 Lie on your back with your arms and legs straight and your palms up.

2 Close your eyes, and breathe deeply.

3 Feel the support of the surface beneath you, and let it completely carry the weight of your body.

4 While you slowly breathe in and out, imagine you are lying on a beach. Using your imagination, see the ocean, the sand, and the blue sky. Hear the waves crash up on the shore. Listen to the seagulls. Feel the warmth of the sand beneath you and the sun shining down on your skin. Smell the salty air and the scent of cocoa-butter lotion. Add any details to your vision that remind you of relaxing at the beach.

5 When you feel ready, breathe deeply, stretch, and open your eyes. You should feel refreshed and relaxed!

Go anywhere!

Remember a favorite place where you were relaxed. Maybe it was your grandmother's kitchen or the spot where you pitched a tent on a camping trip. Replace this beach scene with your special place. Let your imagination take you there whenever you need a break.

Yoga for you

What is it?

Yoga is a practice that includes breathing and exercises (or poses).
Your body and mind work together to build strength, increase
flexibility, improve balance, and provide a sense of peace. Yoga is
an ancient practice thousands of years old, but if you think it's
old-fashioned, think again. More and more people are turning to
yoga for fun, fitness, and relaxation. Find out if it's for you, too!

Getting started

Try the techniques on pages 52 through 61. Then, to find out more about yoga, check out books and videos from your local library. If you'd really like to learn how to do yoga, it's best to learn from a pro. Talk to your mom or gym teacher about finding a class that's right for you.

When doing yoga, remember to:

 find a quiet spot.

 wear loose clothes.

 go barefoot so that you won't slip.

 use a sticky yoga mat for cushioning.

 practice on an empty stomach
(wait an hour if you've eaten a meal).

move in slow motion.

breathe deeply.

Belly breathing is done throughout a yoga workout—while you stretch and warm up, practice poses, and cool down. But try it anytime. Since breathing deeply gets more oxygen to your brain, it'll help you relax.

Just breathe...

You probably think that breathing is easy. You do it automatically. But you might be surprised how different taking a breath can feel if you concentrate. Here's how to do a deep yoga-style breath:

1 Place your hands over your belly.

2 Imagine that there's a balloon in your belly and that the balloon's opening is in your throat.

3 Inhale slowly, filling the balloon from your belly all the way up to your throat. As you inhale, feel your hands rise as your belly expands and your lungs fill with air.

4 Pause and hold the breath for a few seconds.

5 Exhale, letting all the air out of your "balloon." Notice your hands fall as your belly presses in to squeeze out every bit of air.

Take five or six deep breaths in this way.

Cat pose

When you practice this posture, imagine a cat stretching after a nap.

1 Start on your hands and knees with your hands under your shoulders and your knees under your hips. Palms should be flat on the floor, and your toes should point backward.

2 Breathe in. When you exhale, arch your back upward with your head dropping down and your tailbone tucked in. Pull your belly in toward your spine.

3 Pause for a moment or two in this position.

4 When you inhale again, curve your back in the opposite direction, so that your head and tailbone are curving upward.

5 Repeat steps 2 through 4 five times smoothly, with movement following your breath.

Tip: As you do each pose, remember to practice your breathing. If a muscle feels tense, imagine your breath moving directly into the muscle and filling it with relaxation.

Tip: If your floor is slippery, do standing poses on a yoga mat.

Tree pose

While you hold this posture, imagine that your standing leg is the trunk of a tree, with roots growing into the earth, and your arms are the tree's branches.

1. Start by standing tall with your feet together and your arms at your sides.

2. Breathe in, shifting your weight onto your left leg.

3. As you breathe out, bring your right foot up and turn your right knee out to the side. Rest your right foot as high as you can on the inside of your left leg. This may take some practice, so don't worry if you lose your balance. Just move slowly back into position.

4. Try raising your hands straight out from your sides. If you feel balanced, inhale and reach your hands all the way up so that your palms meet overhead.

5. Hold the pose for a count of ten. As you breathe out, return your right foot to the floor. Repeat the pose on your other side.

Warrior 2 pose

Feel strong and confident as you stand in the Warrior 2 pose.

1 Begin with feet together and hands at your sides. Step your feet wide apart.

2 Turn your left foot slightly in to the right. Turn your right foot 90 degrees to the right so that it points straight out to the side. Your hips should stay centered, and your front heel should be in line with the arch of your back foot.

3 Slowly bend your right knee until your knee is directly over your ankle. To protect your knee, be sure you can see your toes.

4 Raise your arms out to the sides. Keep your shoulders relaxed. Turn your head to the right and look out over your fingers.

5 Focus on a spot in front of you and breathe. Take four or five deep breaths, then lower your arms and bring your legs together.

6 Repeat the pose on the other side.

Cobra pose

Feel your chest open and your spine become more flexible with this pose.

1 Lie facedown on the floor. Keep your legs together with the tops of your feet on the floor. Place your hands on the floor under your shoulders, keeping your elbows close to your body.

2 Inhale and, pressing into your hands, slowly raise your head and chest as high as they will comfortably go. Tighten your buttocks muscles to protect your lower back. Press your head up and chest out. Keep your shoulders down and elbows in.

3 Breathe several times, gazing ahead at a point of focus.

4 Exhale as you lower yourself back down to the floor.

big
TRUTH

Life is filled with ups and downs.

You are going
to be here.

You are
here.

If you're feeling down, an up is just around the corner.

When you face a challenge, tell yourself you are strong and smart.
Confidence in yourself will help you keep your cool.

Try to step back and look at the big picture. Change is going to
happen, but you'll be able to handle it with real spirit.

Write to us!

Do you have a favorite way to relax?

How do you unwind after a tough day?

What's your secret to keeping calm in a crisis?

Send your ideas to:

Real Spirit Editor

American Girl

P.O. Box 620998

8400 Fairway Place

Middleton, WI 53562

Here are some other American Girl books you might like:

☐ *I read it.*

☐ *I read it.*

☐ *I read it.*

☐ *I read it.*

☐ *I read it.*

☐ *I read it.*